FACT OR FICTION?

A DOSSIER ON OLD BELIEFS THAT DIE HARD

The Reader's Digest Association Limited London

Fact or Fiction?

Compiled by Russell Ash

Printed in Great Britain

Believing the impossible

As scientific knowledge increases, we have less need of superstition. A primitive tribe may believe that thunder is caused by the bellowing of a giant god, or that a fever can be cured by ritual, but modern man knows better.

And yet as superstitious beliefs slip away we are still left with a core of beliefs which on investigation turn out to be as irrational as those of primitive man. Even history books, magazines, and rumours spread by otherwise intelligent people continue to convey many misconceptions as 'facts'. And because they are long established or exciting, they are believed.

Many delusions that are still clung to – such as the belief that thunder turns milk sour and that a drowning man goes under three times – were deeply rooted long before scientists proved them to be false. We continue to give credence to many historical errors because they demonstrate the traits of a historical character – Nero probably did not fiddle while Rome burnt, but if we think of Nero as an evil man, it is logical that he should have done such a wicked thing. Other beliefs have become accepted parts of the language – the idea, for instance, that an ostrich sticks its head in the sand is a useful metaphor for self-deceiving ignorance, and so we may not even pause to question it. It may be saddening to deflate cherished delusions, but it is a useful lesson in clear thinking to recognise them as 'old wives' tales'. It is easy, as Alice's Queen said, to believe in impossible things, but it is important we should be aware that they are impossible: *Alice laughed. 'There's no use trying,' she said: 'One can't believe impossible things.' 'I daresay you haven't had much practice,' said the Queen. 'When I was your age, I always did it for half-an-hour a day. Why, sometimes I've believed as many as six impossible things before breakfast.'* (Lewis Carroll *Through the Looking-Glass* – 1872)

HISTORY

William of Normandy was named 'The Conqueror' after the Battle of Hastings

William, Duke of Normandy, was called 'The Great' by his contemporaries, but much later he became known as 'Conquaester', which has since come to be translated as the 'Conqueror'.

In fact, William believed he had every right to the English throne – he had been promised it by Edward the Confessor, and had a Bull from Pope Alexander II declaring him the rightful successor. His victory at Hastings, therefore, was held to be the making good of a legal right by occupation – not a conquest by an invading army. 'Conquaester' in this context meant 'acquirer' of the lands of England, not 'vanquisher'.

Cinderella wore glass slippers

Every child knows that in the fairy story Cinderella wore glass slippers and, if impractical, the idea of wearing such delicate footwear is in keeping with the fantastic nature of the tale. But in fact, in the early French version of the story, Cinderella was equipped with far more practical *pantoufles en vair* – slippers of fur or white ermine – a valuable material used only by royalty, and thus appropriate to Cinderella's new-found status. By the 14th century, however, the word *vair* had gone out of use, and so when Charles Perrault re-wrote the story in French in 1697, he was unfamiliar with it, and mistook *vair* for *verre*, or glass.

There have been at different times, amazingly, over 300 forms of the Cinderella story in different countries. In many versions the slipper is made of some scarce material – it is silk, pearl-embroidered, jewel-spangled, silver or gold – but in only six versions is the slipper of glass, and all six are of French origin. We have our version in English from Perrault, and so to us Cinderella's slipper will always be made of glass.

Dick Turpin rode from London to York in a day

The highwayman Dick Turpin (1705–39) is reported to have ridden nearly 200 miles from London to York between morning and evening – a feat believed to be impossible. According to the story, he had committed a robbery near London and raced to York to establish an alibi. But 30 years before Turpin was born, Daniel Defoe wrote that another highwayman, William Nevison, had done exactly the same thing. Defoe wrote of the achievement in his *A Tour thro' the Whole Island of Great Britain.* Lord Macaulay, the historian, was convinced that the story was an old legend which

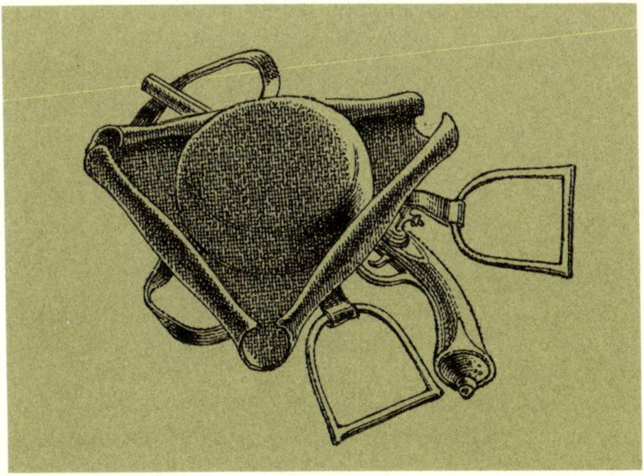

became credited to any rogue of the day – Turpin merely happened to have captured the public's imagination.

It was not Turpin's boldness or brave exploits which made his name endure as Britain's most notorious highwayman. He was a murderous rogue who was eventually captured at York and hanged, like many hundreds of others at that time. His rise to stardom came when he was made the hero of William Harrison Ainsworth's highly successful novel *Rookwood* (1834). Turpin's horse Black Bess was Ainsworth's invention. It was never mentioned in any of the contemporary accounts of Turpin's life.

Christ's feet were nailed to the Cross

There is no Biblical authority for supposing that Christ's feet, as well as his hands, were nailed to the Cross. None of the Gospels gives any details of how Christ was fixed to the Cross and it is only in the Gospel According to John that the nail wounds are mentioned – and then only wounds in the hands. When Christ appeared before the disciples after the Resurrection 'he showed them his hands and his side'. The disciple Thomas, who was not present at this meeting, refused to believe that Christ had risen. He said: 'Unless I see in his hands the print of the nails, and place my finger in the marks of the nails, and place my hand in his side, I will not believe.' Later, Christ appeared before the disciples again and said to Thomas: 'Put your finger here, and see my hands; and put out your hand, and place it in my side; do not be faithless but believing.'

In Luke's Gospel, Jesus appears before the disciples after rising from his tomb and says: 'Why are you troubled, and why do questionings rise in your hearts? See my hands and my feet, that is I myself; handle me and see; for a spirit has no flesh and bones as you see that I have.' No wounds are mentioned, however, and the reference to hands and feet was probably a way of drawing attention to his physical resurrection.

Methods of crucifixion in Roman times varied in different areas, but one common practice was for the hands to be nailed and the feet to be tied in position on a wooden support projecting from the cross.

'Ye' is pronounced 'Yee'

It is common practice to read such signs as 'Ye Olde Tea Shoppe' as '*Yee* Olde . . .' But the correct pronunciation is simply 'the'. This is because in Anglo-Saxon writing the sound 'th' was represented by a symbol known as the thorn, þ, which was later printed as a 'y', though still pronounced 'th'. 'Ye', the plural of 'thou', is however correctly pronounced 'yee'.

Sandwiches were invented by the Earl of Sandwich

Legend has it that John Montagu, the 4th Earl of Sandwich (1718–92), was such a gambler that he would sit for 24 hours at the card table and, rather than halt for food, would have meat brought to him between two slices of bread. Thus the 'sandwich' was born. The actual invention is said by one writer to date from 5 a.m. on August 6, 1762.

But it seems unlikely that throughout centuries of bread-eating in all the countries of the world, no one before 1762 should have hit upon the idea of wrapping a couple of slices of bread round a piece of meat; surely it was just a name for the snack which was lacking? And closer investigation shows this to be the case, for the Romans ate just such a meal, which they called 'offula'. It took many centuries, and the anecdote about Montagu, to provide a name for it in English. However, Montagu's modern biographer says that even the anecdote is incorrect. Apparently, Montagu had no great interest in cards; he was a hard-working statesman, at one time First Lord of the Admiralty, who often ate a 'sandwich' held in one hand while he wrote with the other. News of his habit probably led to the adoption of the word, which was in common use in England from about 1762 onwards.

St George was an English saint who slew a dragon

According to an old English ballad, St George was the son of Lord Albert of Coventry. He fought in the Crusades and while in the Middle East saved Sabra, a king's daughter, from sacrifice to a terrible dragon, which he slew. He then married Sabra and returned with her to live in Coventry.

St George has since become the patron saint of England and several other countries, including Portugal, and also the patron saint of soldiers and Boy Scouts. But what little evidence there is to support his existence suggests that he was actually a soldier of the 3rd–4th century who lived in the Middle East, and was persecuted for his Christian beliefs. He was apparently beheaded about AD 303 by the Roman Emperor Diocletian at Nicomedia (now Izmit) in Turkey. Within 100 years he was being revered throughout the Christian world – including England by the 7th century – as a minor saint. The Crusaders under Richard I believed that he aided them in battle, and when they returned to England at the end of the 12th century they encouraged his adoption as a saint of higher rank. Within a few years his feast day (April 23) was being regularly kept, and about 1348 Edward III dedicated the Order of the Garter to him. His position as patron saint of England stems from about this time. The Roman Catholic Church has recently 'demoted' him (in the sense that his feast day is now observed optionally) because the evidence for his existence is so tenuous.

The story of St George's conquest of the dragon does not figure at all in the earliest accounts of his life, but gradually appeared and gained favour in the Middle Ages. The battle symbolises the conquest of evil, or Satan (the dragon), by good, or Christ (represented by the saint), thus rescuing the faith (the virgin who is to be sacrificed to the dragon). St George's battle has been given an English setting in some versions of the story – such as at Dragon's Hill in Berkshire.

Christ was born on Christmas Day

No one knows the year, let alone the day, when Christ was born. The Gospel of Matthew states that it was 'in the days of Herod'; Luke that it was at the time of Caesar Augustus's tax census. From this and from other evidence Bible historians have placed it anywhere between what we now call 8 BC and AD 6. The establishment of the calendar dating from the supposed year of the birth of Christ is thus fairly arbitrary.

Christmas – the 'Mass of Christ' – was first celebrated a few hundred years after his death, at widely differing dates in January, March, April or September, according to local custom. Eventually it was fixed at December 25, largely because that date coincided with existing pagan festivities which took place towards the year's end – such as Saturnalia, and the 'Dies Natalis Invicti Solis' (Birthday of the Unconquered Sun) which the Romans celebrated, and the ancient Yule festival of northern Europe. The Eastern Orthodox Church, using a different system of calculation, fixed Christmas at January 6.

Two important Christmas traditions are often erroneously believed to have been established in England for centuries – Father Christmas and Christmas trees. Father Christmas, or Santa Claus, is our version of Saint Nicholas, and was introduced into England from the Continent in the 19th century. Christmas trees were used in parts of Europe hundreds of

years ago, and were introduced by German settlers into America in the 18th century. Although their use was known in England in the early 19th century, it was not until Queen Victoria married the German Prince Albert in 1840, and it was reported that they had a tree at the Palace, that the custom of the Christmas tree became widespread.

Marie Antoinette said, 'Let them eat cake'

Hearing that the ordinary people of France had no bread, Marie Antoinette, the ill-fated queen of Louis XVI, is said to have remarked, 'Let them eat cake'. This callous phrase is often quoted as proof of how out of touch the monarchy was with its subjects.

However, a similar story is told in Jean Jacques Rousseau's *Confessions*, written in the 1760's – years before Marie Antoinette arrived in France as the Dauphin's bride. Rousseau attributes the statement to an anonymous 'great princess'.

So if Marie Antoinette did say it, she was not the first, and it is more probable that it was merely ascribed to her by her opponents. (Actually, in Rousseau's version, the 'great princess' was supposed to have said, 'Let them eat *brioche*' – a kind of rich, doughy roll.)

Whatever her views on the peasants' diet, Marie Antoinette was guillotined in 1793, nine months after her husband.

George Washington confessed to cutting down his father's cherry tree

The story of George Washington and the cherry tree is familiar to everyone, even if they know nothing else about American history. Young George, it was said, was given an axe with which he chopped down his father's prized cherry tree. When confronted, George declared that he could not tell a lie, he had indeed felled the tree. The story vouches for the scrupulous honesty of America's first president – although, since he was caught almost red-handed, some cynics have remarked that he could hardly have denied it. However, very little is known of Washington's boyhood, and the tale seems to be no more than a fictitious anecdote. It was first related after Washington's death, in a highly successful biography of him by Mason Locke Weems, known as Parson Weems. The Parson said that he had heard the story some 20 years before from an 'aged lady', a distant relative of Washington. Weems was an imaginative writer who placed little store on historical accuracy. In his life of William Penn, the founder of Pennsylvania, he invented the story of a treaty between the Indians and settlers, complete with quotations, and he was wont to describe himself as 'former rector of Mt Vernon Parish' – which never existed.

Even Weems never said that Washington chopped down the cherry tree – according to him, George merely damaged it badly so that it died. The fact that George is supposed to have been just six years old when the incident occurred, and the flowery language of Weems, makes the following extract a little hard to believe:

'I can't tell a lie, Pa; you know I can't tell a lie. I did cut it down with my hatchet.' 'Run to my arms, you dearest boy' cried his father in transports, 'run to my arms; glad I am, George, that you killed my tree; for you have paid me for it a thousand fold. Such an act of heroism in my son is more worth than a thousand trees, though blossomed with silver and their fruits of purest gold.'

(M. L. Weems *Life of George Washington* 10th edition, 1810)

Richard III was a hunchback

Shakespeare, in the play *Richard III*, refers repeatedly to the king's alleged deformity. Shakespeare, and presumably his audience, had no doubts that Richard was a grotesque monster who had seized the throne illegally and murdered the Princes in the Tower. But Shakespeare was writing for a Tudor audience, and using Tudor historical materials – and the Tudors had every reason to discredit Richard III, the last Plantagenet king, and establish their own right to the throne. After Henry VII, the first Tudor monarch, overthrew Richard at Bosworth, the Tudors began an elaborate character assassination, so that he emerges even today as a kind of devil incarnate.

However his hump back is not mentioned by any contemporary chronicler except one – who violently opposed Richard – and he overstated his case by including such other defects as a withered arm. After his death, when the poison pens were in full flow, Richard acquired 'one shoulder higher than the other', and this is followed by all sorts of gruesome, and obviously fictitious tales concerning his birth – such as that he was two years in his mother's womb because nature could not face the idea of his being unleashed upon the world. But a Silesian traveller, Nicolas von Poppelau, who saw Richard, was much impressed by his appearance. Contemporary portraits do not show him to have been anything but normal, and his armour and his known skill in jousting are not consistent with a deformed man.

The 'Sargasso Sea' traps ships in seaweed

Travellers' tales and accounts in literature from the time of Columbus abound in references to the 'Sargasso Sea' – a section of the Atlantic Ocean so choked with seaweed that ships are unable to proceed through it, and in which many vessels have become trapped. It has even been identified with the legendary lost kingdom of Atlantis. Its name derives from Columbus's name for it – 'Mar de Sargaço' – the sea of seaweed.

However, these tales are greatly exaggerated. In 1910–11, a Norwegian research ship, the *Michael Sars*, searched in vain for the Sargasso Sea. The crew found, as many sailors had before, an expanse of sea below the 40th Parallel, between the Azores and Charleston, South Carolina, where the conditions are favourable for the growth of *Sargassum bacciferum* and other species of seaweed and floating algae. But there is no 'submerged meadow', and no danger to ships which enter the zone.

The guillotine was invented during the French Revolution by Dr Guillotin

The guillotine is always associated with the French Revolution, and the natural assumption is that its invention dates from that time. This is not correct. The earliest form of a beheading machine of this type dates from the medieval period. Holinshead, the historian much studied by Shakespeare, reports that a beheading machine was used in Ireland in 1307. The National Museum of Antiquities in Edinburgh has a fearful early version of the guillotine, known as the 'Maiden'. It was used in Edinburgh in 1581 to execute the Regent, James Morton, for his part in the murder of Darnley, the husband of Mary, Queen of Scots. Morton himself is said to have gained the idea for the 'Maiden' after seeing a similar device in England. The English 'guillotine' was called the 'Halifax Gibbet'. Holinshead, writing in 1572, says that since ancient times the machine had been used in Halifax to behead thieves found guilty of stealing property worth more than 'thirteen-pence half-penny'. The executions took place on the market day after conviction. The harsh verdicts of the Halifax assizes led to the expression 'From Hull, Hell and Halifax, Good Lord, deliver us' (Hull being an inhospitable town for beggars).

In England and on the Continent, this and similar machines had fallen out of use by the 18th century. In France at this time, the nature of torture and execution depended on the class of the victim – aristocrats alone had the privilege of being beheaded. In the egalitarian spirit of the Revolution, and in the interests of humanity, Dr Joseph Ignace Guillotin proposed in 1789 the introduction of a 'simple mechanism' to execute all convicted of a capital offence, irrespective of class. His idea probably came from a written account of an execution in Milan in 1702, when a similar machine was used. Dr Guillotin described to the National Assembly how 'the mechanism falls like lightning, the head flies, the man is no more'. His proposals were greeted with laughter, but gradually his ideas gained favour, and by 1792 the first machine had been built. Although Guillotin was consulted, the design was the work of Dr Antoine Louis of the Academy of Surgery, and the construction was carried out by Tobias Schmidt, a German piano-maker. Its first trials took place at Bicetre hospital in Paris, which was then a mental asylum, using the dead bodies of patients. Within weeks a highwayman named Pelletier became its first live victim. At first, the machine was called the 'louisette' and other names, but 'guillotine' was soon adopted. In the whole of France during the Revolution, some 17,000 aristocrats and 'enemies of the Revolution' died on the guillotine.

The blade from an early guillotine – possibly the one used to execute Louis XVI – is now in the collection of Madame Tussaud's in London. It has the famous slanted edge, unlike the Edinburgh 'Maiden' whose blade is square. In his novel, *Philip*, Thackeray asks: 'Was not good Dr Guillotin executed by his own invention?' Although this was widely believed, the answer is no – Guillotin lived on through the Revolution, dying in 1814 at the age of 76, of a carbuncle of the shoulder.

'Sirloin' originated when a king jokingly knighted a joint of beef

Writers in every century since the 17th have accredited the origin of the word 'sirloin' to a king of 100 years or so before, who, on a whim, dubbed a piece of beef with his sword and said: 'Arise, Sir-loin.' In fact 'sirloin' comes from the Old French, *sur loigne*, or the 'over loin' of beef.

Lady Godiva rode naked through Coventry

There undoubtedly was a Lady Godiva – she was the wife of Leofric, an 11th-century baron who lived through the reigns of Cnut and Edward the Confessor. Both she and her husband were buried at the abbey church of Coventry. Leofric, the story goes, imposed a crippling tax on the town. When his wife begged him to withdraw it, he jokingly said he would do so when she had ridden naked through the streets. Lady Godiva took him at his word and Leofric honoured the bargain. No one saw Godiva on her ride except 'Peeping Tom' who was struck blind by heavenly intervention. The tale is unique, simple and dramatic, and although there is no firm reason to believe it really occurred, there are also no grounds for supposing it did not. The legend was first told by the prior, Roger of Wendover, at the end of the 12th century. Some historians have suggested that he misunderstood a story of her 'stripping herself' of her possessions, or that it was actually the horse that was naked – that is, it was denuded of all badges of rank, and Lady Godiva was thus humbling herself to win the bargain with Leofric. What is certain is that Peeping Tom played no part; he was not introduced into the story until several hundred years later.

Cleopatra killed herself with an asp

The account of Cleopatra's dramatic death in 30 BC – by clasping a poisonous snake to her bosom – has often been repeated, by Shakespeare and other writers. But we have no way of knowing the truth. The early Greek historian

Plutarch merely says that 'some relate' that to be the manner of her death, but he offers other, less thrilling conjectures. It is said she had a hollow bodkin in her hair, and that in it she hid poison which she may have taken after the defeat and suicide of her lover Mark Antony. But after her death it was rumoured that a basket of figs had been delivered to her containing, according to her orders, an asp. Two small marks were said to have been found on her left arm – not her bosom – which could have been caused by a snake bite.

The victorious Roman general, Octavian, ordered an immediate inquest, and apparently summoned 'psylly' – men who were believed to have the power to suck poison from bodies and thus revive them – but to no avail. Eventually, when Octavian rode in triumph through Rome, a chariot followed him with a statue of Cleopatra lying dead on her couch. Entwined around her left arm was a model of an asp, and that may have started further rumours concerning her suicide. But it is important to consider that the asp was also a symbol of Egyptian royalty.

A Dutch boy saved a town by putting his finger in a hole in the dyke

One of the classic tales of youthful heroism is that of the little Dutch boy who, though numb with cold, kept his finger in a hole in a leaking dyke until help arrived, and so saved the town of Haarlem (some say the whole of Holland) from being flooded. But anyone who looks for the origin of the story in Dutch history will look in vain. It was the invention of a 19th-century American writer of children's fiction, Mary Mapes Dodge, and it first appeared in some – but, curiously, not all – editions of her book *Hans Brinker, or the Silver Skates*, published over 100 years ago. As the lad spots the hole and plugs it with his 'chubby little finger', he gives 'a chuckle of boyish delight', and says, 'the angry waters must stay back now! Haarlem shall not be drowned while *I* am here!' Almost as if in anticipation of accusations of fabricating history, Miss Dodge has one of her characters remark: 'True? Of course it is . . . there is not a child in Holland who does not know it.' Finally, even Holland has adopted this fictitious tale; the nameless hero is commemorated by a statue to him unveiled in 1950 at Spaarndam Lock.

Boadicea used scythes on her chariot wheels

It seems doubtful that Boadicea, the 1st century AD queen of the Iceni (who inhabited what is now East Anglia) really did use scythes on the axles of her chariots, although illustrations of all kinds, including the statue of her beside Westminster Bridge, perpetuate this belief. Scythes could not have been discriminating – they would have hacked at the legs of her own warriors and horses equally with those of the Romans. Also, there is no archaeological evidence to show that such weapons existed at any time. Even if the scythes existed they cannot have been very effective; it is said that with an army of only 10,000 Suetonius Paulinus was able decisively to defeat Boadicea's army of 200,000.

English witches were burnt at the stake

In Germany, where the persecution of witches in the 15th to 17th centuries was very severe, thousands of people accused of witchcraft were burnt at the stake after undergoing all manner of cruel tortures. In Scotland, too, some were burnt alive, although it was customary for witches to be strangled before their bodies were burnt. It is, however, a mistake to suppose that burning alive was the penalty for witches in England or America, where the usual punishment was hanging. In England, there were several other crimes for which burning was a punishment, and under an Act passed during the reign of Henry VIII poisoning was treason, and punishable by 'deth by boylynge'. A wife who murdered her husband was guilty of petty treason and could be burnt at the stake, as could a heretic. But there are no legal records of any witches officially being burnt in England or America for witchcraft alone, although there may have been isolated cases of burnings by lynch-law.

After the witchcraft trials at Salem, Massachusetts, in 1692, 19 people were hanged and one man was pressed to death with weights.

King John signed the Magna Carta

This simple statement, although it appears in almost all school history books, is incorrect; John did not sign the document – he *sealed* it. And he may not even have done that personally. It is even doubtful that he could write;

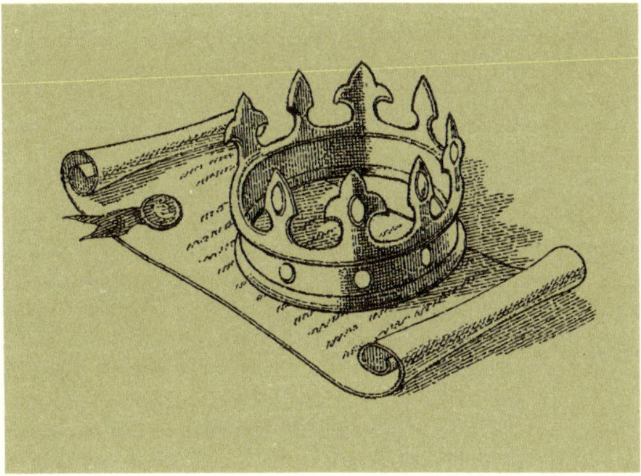

certainly, there are no samples of his handwriting in existence anywhere. The seal was a round piece of wax, about 4 in. in diameter, imprinted with images of King John on both sides and hung from the document by a parchment tag.

The original Magna Carta no longer exists, although a manuscript known as the Articles of the Barons, which formed the basis of the Magna Carta, is in the British Museum. The British Museum also has two copies of the original – one of which still bears traces of the seal. (There are two further contemporary copies – in Lincoln and Salisbury Cathedrals.)

William Tell shot an apple from his son's head

Everyone knows the story of William Tell, who refused to salute Governor Gessler's cap, placed in a Swiss market-place as a symbol of the Hapsburg Imperial rule over Switzerland in the 14th century. Tell (whose surname, incidentally, means 'the mad') was seized and ordered to shoot an apple perched on his son's head. He succeeded, but Gessler demanded to know why he had with him a second arrow. When Tell replied that it was to kill Gessler if his son had been injured, he was taken in chains across a lake to Kussnacht Castle. However he managed to escape from the boat – his 'leap' is still shown to tourists. He then shot Gessler, led a resistance movement which liberated Switzerland and, eventually, after many adventures, died at Schachenbach. Even the date given to the apple incident – November 18, 1307 – adds apparent historical accuracy to the story. But historians have found no evidence to support it.

There is no mention in any contemporary Swiss record of anyone by the name of William Tell or Gessler - indeed so unhistorical is the story believed to be that in 1890 Schwyz Canton in Switzerland directed that it should be cut out of all the history books being used in the canton's schools.

Tales of amazing feats of archery involving sons date back to ancient Greece, and also occur in British folklore. In the north of England, William of Cloudesly is commemorated in an old ballad for shooting an apple from his son's head at 120 paces. A Scottish archer in South Uist, Black-haired Gilpatrick, is reputed to have shot an egg from his son's head at 100 yds. He also had a second arrow in his belt for his chief, MacDonald of Clanranald, who had ordered him to attempt the shot.

Dark-skinned inhabitants of Britain are descendants of Spanish Armada sailors

This is a strongly rooted belief, and in the Orkneys people with dark wavy hair are still called 'Dons'. But it is quite without foundation. There are certainly dark-skinned and dark-haired people in Scotland, Ireland and Cornwall, but they are almost all of Celtic origin and have predominantly grey eyes – not the characteristic brown of the inhabitants of Spain and Portugal. None has a Spanish name, which one might expect to have been perpetuated in the male line, and no families of long standing in these areas can produce evidence of a Spanish pedigree. Also, the number of shipwrecked Armada sailors was small, and most of the few who reached land eventually found their way back to their own countries. Even if any did settle in Britain, their descendants would not be sufficient to affect the physical makeup of present generations.

MEDICINE

Julius Caesar was born by caesarian operation

Until the invention of antiseptics in recent times, caesarian section – the 'emergency exit' technique employed in cases of difficult childbirth – was a highly risky, although not impossible, operation. It was certainly known in the Ancient World, but it is most probable that although some babies may have been saved in this way the mothers would have died of septicaemia and other complications. We know, however, that Julius Caesar's mother, Aurelia, did not die – she was certainly alive when Caesar invaded Britain in 55 BC. If he had been born by caesarian section, it is surprising that it is not mentioned by the notable Roman doctor Celsus, who wrote of the operation in detail in AD 30. Somewhat later, however, the untrustworthy historian Pliny does suggest that Caesar was born by this method.

Confusion could have occurred over the Latin word *caesura*, a cut; but there is an even more likely explanation. Under a Roman law, women who died in late pregnancy were operated on to remove the child – possibly to save it, but also so that mother and child could be buried separately. The law was known as the *lex caesarea*, and was codified about 700 years before the time of Julius Caesar. Children born in this way were known as *caesones*. Caesarian may thus have derived from the name of the law which demanded it, and which was in no way connected with Caesar.

The first successful operation for child *and* mother was said to have been performed by the Swiss Jacob Nufer in 1500, but the evidence for any operation before the 18th century is very scanty. It was not until the early 17th century that the term caesarian was first used in English, although the technique was clearly familiar to Shakespeare – in *Macbeth*, Macduff was 'from my mother's womb untimely ripp'd'. It was, however, extremely dangerous until this century; even in the 19th century, a mortality rate for the mothers of 75 per cent was recorded. Now caesarian section is an important and safe method of delivering babies.

People falling from great heights are dead before they hit the ground

Despite the evidence to the contrary, the myth of mid-air death persists. There are numerous cases on record where people have fallen from high buildings and have by some means escaped death, without any suggestion of even loss of consciousness. There is, on the other hand, no evidence to suggest that people who have been killed by falls were dead prior to their impact with the ground. Free-fall parachutists often fall several miles and attain a maximum velocity of

over 120 mph without suffering any ill effects. Before such leaps, it was popularly held that the sheer speed of the descent would kill (in fact, it was once believed that such great speeds as 25 mph on the early railways would prove fatal), and that it was impossible to breathe during a sustained fall.

Some remarkable escapes from great falls have been recorded. In 1800, a steeplejack fell 120 ft from the Church of St George, Bolton-le-Moors, denting some sheet metal on the ground with his head. He got up and walked away, unharmed.

One of the most amazing falls occurred in 1944 when RAF tail-gunner Nicholas Alkemade leapt from a blazing Lancaster bomber over Germany without his parachute. He fell 18,000 ft into a fir tree which broke his fall, and landed in a snowdrift without being injured.

Motorway bridges contain the bodies of dead workmen

When work began on the numerous motorway bridges in England, a rumour soon circulated that workmen had been somehow entombed in the concrete. The stories were often embellished by mention of sophisticated X-ray equipment which had allegedly been used (always in vain) to locate the bodies. It was seldom stated whether the workmen found their way into the concrete by accident or design; and although the stories were said to stem from eye-witness accounts, none of the eye-witnesses had, curiously, ever attempted to rescue their colleagues.

There can be no doubt that there is little substance in these tales, which perhaps arose when workers for some reason failed to report for duty. Similar tales have cropped up in many other countries – in the USA, for example, it is popularly supposed that victims of Mafia executions are disposed of by being entombed in concrete river piers. When accidents have occurred on construction sites, strenuous efforts have been made to rescue survivors and recover bodies – as in the case of a bridge collapse near Pasadena, California, on October 17, 1972, when a body was actually recovered from a 100 ton block of cement – and it is very unlikely that any genuine suspicion that a worker had fallen into a mass of concrete would go unheeded.

Powdered glass is a poison

It is curious that the belief in the efficacy of powdered glass as a murder weapon should have come about, since in early times it was actually believed to have medicinal properties. But its use as a 'slow poison' was firmly established by the 17th century, when Sir Thomas Browne, a British scientist and antiquarian, tried to disprove it:

> 'That glass is a poison, according unto common conceit, I know not how to grant . . . having given dogs above a dram thereof, subtilly powdered in butter and paste, without any visible disturbance'
>
> (*Pseudoxia Epidemica* – 1646)

In this century, several trials have taken place in cases which involved the use of powdered glass, but no one has been convicted of murder by this means. In a case in the early part of the century, a doctor called as an expert witness said he would gladly swallow powdered glass in court; and in a murder case at Ilford in 1922, the defendant, a Mrs Thompson, admitted to having tried to kill her husband with powdered glass, but without success.

Glass which is powdered finely enough to be concealed in food, and thus eaten unawares, is too fine to have any ill effects on the digestive system; the stomach and intestines are stronger than most people imagine, and can well cope with much foreign matter, including the grit from stone-ground flour and dirt from unwashed vegetables. Large and possibly dangerous splinters of glass would undoubtedly be noticed before they were swallowed. Powdered glass, if swallowed, could only cause serious injury if it were absorbed into the lungs.

Rubber boots 'draw the feet'

It is often said that rubber boots 'draw the feet' – that is, they exert some kind of sucking effect and thus drain moisture from the feet. The body actually loses a couple of pints of liquid daily through 'insensible perspiration' – it is not noticed because it evaporates from the entire surface of the skin as it appears. However, rubber boots prevent this evaporation because they are waterproof (leather boots, on the other hand, can 'breathe'), and so the skin feels moister than usual.

Fright cures hiccups

The eccentric English sportsman, John Mytton (1796–1834), nearly killed himself by attempting to cure a bout of hiccups by setting fire to his nightshirt. It is not recorded whether the hiccups went, but if they did, there is no reason to suppose that it was the fright that stopped them. It is also unlikely that any other folk remedies, such as drinking out of 'the wrong side' of a glass or holding the breath, really cure hiccups.

The Guinness Book of Records notes the case of Jack O'Leary of California, who had hiccups for eight years. None of the 60,000 suggested cures he is said to have received worked, until eventually he was cured, apparently by a prayer to St Jude – the patron saint of lost causes. Hiccups are spasms of the diaphragm, caused by a variety of factors, and have a way of disappearing without outside intervention. It is probably safer to wait for an attack to pass, rather than risk any possible effects of a sudden fright; more people have died of fright than of hiccups.

A weak chin shows weakness of character

The idea that a 'weak chin' indicates a weak character is a stereotype repeatedly shown in literature and drama, where foolish aristocrats, for example, are traditionally represented as 'chinless wonders'. The belief probably arose along with the whole pseudo-science of physiognomy – the study of the face to reveal character traits. A weak chin is clearly the opposite of the thrusting jaw associated with 'strong' characters – pugilists, gorillas, bulldogs, etc. But there is absolutely no evidence for the idea that it is a sign of weakness. In fact such forceful personalities as General James Wolfe, the conqueror of Quebec, and the Brontë sisters had receding chins.

Similarly, a 'low forehead' or 'close-set eyes' are no

evidence of criminal tendencies. The head measurements of any group of criminals are unlikely to differ noticeably from those of any other group of the population.

Flowers in a sickroom or bedroom at night are dangerous

It is quite widely held – even among some nurses – that flowers should always be removed from a bedroom at night. This is done in the belief that they release some noxious gas or consume oxygen. They are believed to do these things only at night, never during the day. It has even been suggested that it would be possible to commit suicide merely by sleeping in a room filled with flowers. The belief is probably based on the fact that plants growing in the open air give off oxygen during the day and carbon dioxide at night, in the process of using the energy of sunlight to manufacture food. However, the amounts involved are minute. Provided a room is sufficiently well ventilated, even a large quantity of flowers would make no important difference to the oxygen content. On the other hand, wilting flowers in stale water may be unpleasant in a room at any time.

Florence Nightingale was aware of the error of this belief over 100 years ago, and it seems strange that we should cling to it even today.

Carrots help you see in the dark

Carrots contain a substance called carotene, which is converted by the body into vitamin A. This vitamin A, in turn, aids the formation of visual purple, a pigment in the retina of the eyes which is essential for good vision in poor light – although it does not enable a person to see in total darkness. Second World War pilots were encouraged to eat plenty of carrots, which it was believed would improve their vision

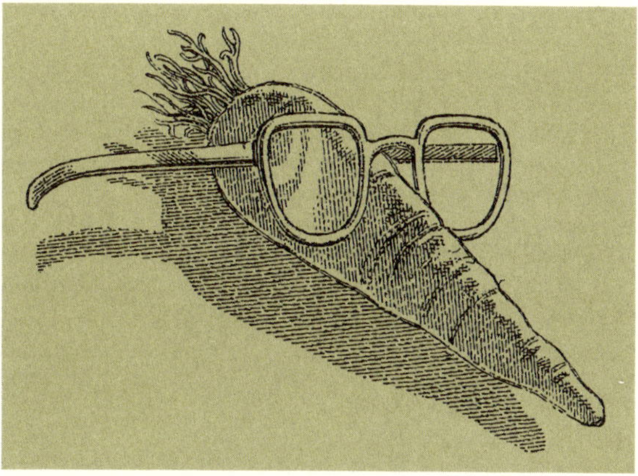

on night missions. Adequate vitamin A is, however, provided by a balanced diet, as it is present in milk, butter and green vegetables, and there is no need to eat carrots to guard against night-blindness.

The heart is on the left side of the body

It is said to be dangerous to sleep on the left side because pressure is exerted on the heart. Pains in the left side of the chest are commonly believed to be symptoms of heart disease. People who are shot in the left breast are invariably killed – Dr No in the James Bond novel miraculously escaped death because he was a 'man in a million' whose heart was on the right. All of this is untrue. The heart, most people are surprised to learn, is more or less dead centre. The left ventricle of the heart, its largest chamber, can be more easily heard on the left, and the largest artery, the aorta, arches to the left. But a vertical section through the middle of the body would slice through the middle of the heart – with maybe an ounce or two more on the left. The heart is certainly not markedly offset. Even if the heart were on the left, sleeping on that side would have no effect, as the rib cage is strong enough to protect it. Chest pains on the left are more likely to be associated with rheumatism or other muscular pains than heart disease, which often produces no symptoms of this kind until a late stage. It has been suggested that as many as half the people who try to commit suicide by shooting or stabbing themselves through the heart actually miss and puncture the left lung.

An apple a day keeps the doctor away

There is some truth in this belief. Apples are a source of vitamin C, which is known to provide resistance to some diseases, and the roughage they contain is beneficial to the intestines. But apples should not be regarded as cure-alls. Plenty of other fruits contain vitamin C – oranges are a much richer source – and roughage can be found in bran, celery and numerous vegetables.

Your past life is recalled in a flash at the moment of death

The idea of an 'action replay' of one's entire past life in the moment before death, especially by drowning, is a much repeated dramatic device. In the film *Two Seconds* (1932), Edward G. Robinson played the part of a convicted murderer, and the film consisted of 'flashbacks' to his life of crime during the two seconds it takes for the electric chair to do its work. There cannot, by definition, be any evidence to support the belief, because anyone who experienced the phenomenon 'at the moment of death' must have died a moment later.

There are numerous cases where people have been saved from the brink of death and have not had any such experience. In most recorded cases they were either unconscious or concerned only with finding some way out of their predicament, or gripped by some fixed idea (such as the effect of their death on their families), or so terrified that their minds were a complete blank.

The theory behind the belief is also difficult to credit. How could the brain select key events from life and compute so rapidly that a mental picture of the entire sequence is registered in a matter of seconds? The brain is also called upon to make a prediction of the future 'moment of death' in order to decide when to begin the lightning playback – which it is not equipped to do.

Hair and nails grow after death

Folklore from earliest times abounds with ghoulish tales of the coffins of clean-shaven or bald men being opened to reveal corpses shrouded in luxuriant hair and beards. Formerly neatly manicured fingernails are reported to have reached Chinese mandarin lengths. The *New York Medical Record* in 1877 carried a report by a Dr Caldwell of Iowa, describing an exhumation which Caldwell said he attended. He claimed that the hair and beard of the previously clean-shaven corpse had burst open the coffin and was growing through the cracks.

Such stories, however, belong to the realm of folklore, for there is absolutely no scientific basis for this belief. The only way in which growth of human tissue can take place is by cell multiplication, and the only way that can occur is for the cells to receive a plentiful supply of oxygen. When the heart and lungs cease to function at death, the body no longer receives oxygen and cellular activity stops. Any independent continuance of hair or nail cell activity would be momentary and certainly immeasurable. The shrinkage of the skin surrounding the hair follicles of the scalp and beard, and that of the fingertips after death might reveal a further 1/16 in. or so of existing hair or nail – but by no means sufficient to burst a lid off a coffin.

You should feed a cold and starve a fever

There is no possible justification for stuffing yourself full of food when you have a cold, or abstaining totally in the case of a fever. The side-effects of over-indulgence or loss of energy which may result in either case are ill-advised additions to the existing symptoms. With either a cold or a fever a reasonable amount of food should be taken. In the case of a flu fever, aspirin and plenty of liquid to replace losses through sweating are also advisable.

Seaside air contains health-giving 'ozone'

Ozone is a colourless gas, first noticed, but not fully understood, in 1785. It is an 'allotrope' – a special form of oxygen consisting of molecules each made up of three atoms, represented by the chemical symbol O_3. Ordinary oxygen has two atoms, and is thus O_2.

Perhaps because to the non-scientist 'O_3' implies an extra share of oxygen atoms it has been assumed that ozone is a super-concentrated form of oxygen, and is thus highly invigorating. For some reason, seaside air is said to contain plenty of ozone. This is possibly due to the vague idea that ozone has a distinctive smell and so does the seaside – but the seaside aroma comes largely from rotting seaweed.

The truth about ozone is alarmingly different from the popular belief. Ozone does have a pungent odour (its name comes from a Greek word which means 'to smell'), but its chemical properties are markedly different from those of oxygen. It is a powerful oxidising agent, readily attacking and destroying metals, rubber and other natural products. It has uses as a powerful germicide, but its chief effect on man is to act as an irritant on the mucous membranes, rather like chlorine, causing the eyes and the nose to stream. Like chlorine, it is positively harmful to breathe.

There is, fortunately, very little ozone in the air, and certainly no more at the seaside than anywhere else; in fact, there is practically none below 8000 ft, as it is formed by the action of lightning on oxygen in the upper atmosphere. To compare the amounts of gases in the atmosphere, if they were separated into layers, inert nitrogen would measure a depth of some 6.2 km, oxygen 1.7 km and ozone about 3 mm.

A pin prick is more dangerous than a prick from a needle

It is popularly believed that a needle piercing the skin is safe, and so a needle is usually selected to remove a splinter from the finger. On the other hand, it is regarded as dangerous to prick the finger with a pin. It was once thought that needles were safe, but pins dangerous because they were made of different metals – but the argument is not valid because metals used for either needles or pins are not poisonous in themselves. What can be dangerous, however, are the germs which may be carried on the point of a pin *or* a needle. A rusty pin is probably dirty and germ-laden, and an infection would be caused by the germs, not the rust; but the same would be true of a dirty needle.

Tooth decay is unknown among primitive people

Explorers often commented on the gleaming white teeth of the primitive peoples they visited – in contrast to the often sad state of teeth in their own countries. It is certainly true that even in the absence of dentistry, toothpaste, and all the paraphernalia of contemporary Western society, the teeth of primitive people still tend to be better than our own. Earlier this century, a comparison of the teeth of 18-year-olds showed that among whites in Western urban areas only 10–15 per cent had perfect teeth; among Zulus, the figure was 89–94 per cent. The cause of this disparity is largely diet. Tooth decay, the most common ailment in Western society, is caused mainly by sugary foods which are less prevalent in primitive areas. However, as soon as 'backward' tribes come into contact with Western man, and begin to eat his diet, their teeth respond in the same way. They have no in-built resistance to tooth decay, and some people have suffered from caries right through history. There is plenty of fossil evidence to show that early man often had toothache – the skull of Rhodesian Man, of 30,000 years ago, contained a full set of teeth, all of which had clearly decayed during his lifetime.

Hair can turn white overnight

History – even relatively modern history – offers numerous stories of people who, due to some sudden or terrible experience, have had their hair turn white 'overnight'. Louis, Duke of Brunswick in the 13th century, is said to have had his wife put to death for infidelity, but when he learnt that she was innocent, his hair turned white 'immediately'. A nameless young man during the reign of Charles V, Emperor of the Holy Roman Empire, was imprisoned for seduction in 1546, and expected to receive the death penalty the next day. His hair and beard were said to have turned grey overnight, and the Emperor was so moved by his plight that he pardoned him. The Boston Medical Journal in the mid-19th century reported the case of a 30-year-old man who was woken at a mining camp by a huge grizzly bear towering over him. The fright allegedly caused his hair to turn white overnight.

Hair can certainly begin quite suddenly to *grow* white or grey as the result of ill-health or various nervous disorders – but it is a gradual process. Hair grows from the roots by continual cell multiplication, but what emerges on the surface is actually dead. No external or internal influences – short of bleach or dye – can affect the colour of hair which has already grown. As hair grows by about ½ in. a month it would take many weeks for a head of hair to 'turn white'. On the other hand, if all a person's hair began to grow white at the same time, the white base of the hair would be noticeable quite quickly.

Fish is good for the brain

During the 19th century, it was discovered that the brain contained phosphorus. The German philosophical writer

Ludwig Buchner, was aware of this when he wrote: 'Without phosphorus, there is no thought.' The French chemist Jean Dumas, showed that fish are a rich source of phosphorus, and Jean Louis Agassiz, the Swiss naturalist and a great authority on fish, connected the two ideas and suggested that eating fish is good for the brain. There may also be an earlier association with the belief that medieval monks, who at one time held a virtual monopoly on learning, derived their 'brain power' from the fish which they traditionally ate.

However, the idea is erroneous, since in adults the phosphorus in the brain does not have to be replenished. Even if it were necessary to 'feed the brain', fish would not be a better source than many other foods, including eggs, milk, meat and poultry, which also contain phosphorus and other essential elements. The brain undergoes its most rapid phase of development in infancy, and all sorts of elements as well as phosphorus are required – and at this stage milk, not fish, forms the staple diet.

Brown eggs are more nutritious than white eggs

Although the colour of the shell in no way affects the contents of an egg, it is commonly believed in England that brown eggs are more nutritious than white, and farmers strive to produce sufficient brown eggs to satisfy the demand. Curiously, however, in some countries, such as the USA, white eggs are believed to be somehow 'purer', and so are more in demand than brown eggs.

Shaving makes hair grow faster

Beard growth, like baldness, is determined by heredity, and cannot be influenced by any external means. Once the hair has emerged from the follicles in which it is produced, it is

dead, and no amount of shaving will speed up its growth.

The belief that repeated shaving when baldness occurs will 'divert energy' from the chin to the scalp is also quite fallacious.

Eyes can be removed and replaced without harm

There is a widespread belief that human eyes can easily be removed and replaced. Stories are frequently repeated of their being somehow 'popped out', lain on the cheek, hanging by the optic nerve, washed and put back without damaging them. However, eyes are held in place by six muscles and are further anchored by the very delicate optic nerve. To remove one without harming the patient would be as impossible as unscrewing his head.

ANIMALS

Wolves hunt in packs, and sometimes rear children

It is an established 'fact' of natural history that wolves always hunt in packs. A pack of wolves is said to be extremely dangerous to man – but there are also supposedly cases where she-wolves have actually reared human babies, such as in the legend of Romulus and Remus, the founders of Rome, and in Kipling's story of Mowgli.

Observers of wolf behaviour have never observed a 'pack' of more than a dozen – certainly nothing of the magnitude of the packs of hundreds which are said to roam the Siberian forests. The wolf is usually a solitary animal – hence the expression 'lone wolf' – and a group of even four or so, which would probably represent a family group, is fairly unusual. A pack of wolves may perhaps be found during severe weather when they may band together to hunt a large animal.

As for the danger of attack by wolves, there are almost no authentic records of such happenings. The Biological Survey in Washington, USA, once investigated all published accounts of wolves killing human beings in the USA and Canada, and could not find a single genuine case.

There are also many stories of wolves rearing children – especially in India. A so-called 'wolf-child' found there in 1926 was said to bark at night, to eat grass and to run on all fours. But the evidence for such tales is extremely thin. What makes them especially suspect is the fact that in the reports 'wolf-children' never act like real wolves, but like the common erroneous idea of a wolf – with drooling fangs, eerie light emitting from the eyes, howling at set intervals, and running in packs. Most telling of all, they have grown pointed canine teeth or their spines have become modified so that they physically resemble wolves – both of which are plainly absurd.

It sometimes rains fish and frogs

The eccentric American Charles Fort, who died in 1932, spent most of his life gathering information concerning unusual downpours of fish, frogs, curious carved stones, hatchets and other remarkable objects. Fort certainly had no problems in finding suitable material, as folklore abounds in tales of such phenomena, which have seemingly been observed in all lands at all times. In England, at Hendon near Sunderland on August 24, 1918, sand eels were said to have rained from the sky and covered about one-third of an acre. According to the Prussian traveller, Humboldt, in 1698 the volcano, Carguairazo, erupted and sprayed boiled catfish over Ecuador. Charles Fort was convinced that there

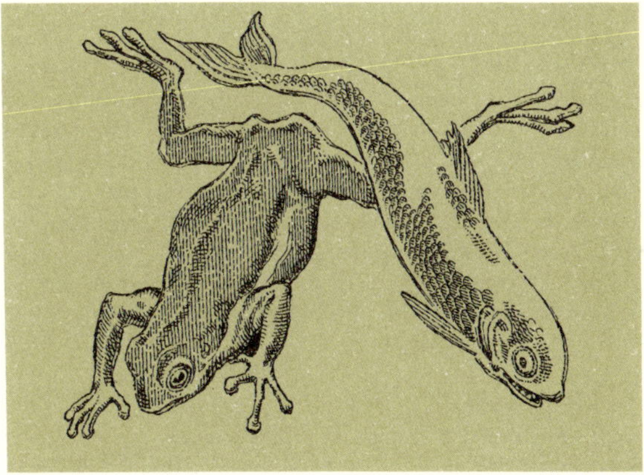

was a sea hovering in the atmosphere 'beyond the earth's gravity', from which living creatures and other objects occasionally fell.

More rational scientific explanations have been put forward, however. In the case of reptiles and amphibians, such as frogs and toads, it seems likely that sudden heavy rains flush them from their hiding places beneath rocks, so that they appear to have come with the rain. Waterspouts from the sea or large lakes may possibly carry with them fish which fall some distance away, and birds may sometimes drop fish which they have caught. There is plenty of sound evidence that fish and other creatures have 'rained' from the sky, and the various means by which they did so have not yet been fully explained.

The phrase 'raining cats and dogs' originates from a quite different source. In Scandinavia the cat is associated with storms and the dog and the wolf with the wind. So 'raining cats and dogs' is an imported expression meaning heavy rain with wind.

Toads cause warts

The warty appearance of some species of toads has led people to believe that they cause warts on the hands if touched. This is not true. Toads release an irritating secretion from their skin which is designed to repel other animals. In contact with a cut on the skin of the hand it would probably cause some itching and discomfort, but it could not cause a wart. In fact, among the gipsies and some South American Indians, it is believed that handling toads cures warts.

Snakes hypnotise their prey

Anyone who believes that snakes have the power to hypnotise or 'fascinate' their prey is in good company, for the same opinion is expressed by the Bible, John Wesley, Shakespeare and Byron, as well as by numerous other writers and travellers. But naturalists have shown that the snake has no such ability. It is true that a snake, having no movable eyelid, can stare fixedly, and no doubt many small animals if confronted by a snake may become motionless with terror. The snake follows the movement of the prey until ready to strike, and naturally the animal stares back, waiting for an opportunity to escape; but no hypnosis is involved.

Monkeys pick fleas from one another's fur

Monkeys in zoos are frequently seen searching themselves and their neighbours, and putting the findings into their mouths. It is usually assumed that they are searching for fleas and they probably are: monkeys in captivity are less likely to have fleas and other parasites than monkeys in the wild. The fact that they continue the habit indicates that it is also

a form of social behaviour – and apparently particles of salt produced by the skin and loose flakes of dried skin are as good to eat as fleas.

Swans sing before dying

The swan, though not totally mute, does not make any sound which can be remotely compared with singing. Yet it has been believed since earliest times that just before they die, swans will burst into sweet song. From this idea we have derived the expression 'swan song', used by Shakespeare and numerous poets.

The belief seems to date from classical times, when a Greek legend told how the soul of Apollo, God of Music, entered a swan. Socrates, in Plato's *Phaedo*, says that they sing, 'Not out of sorrow or distress, but because they are inspired of Apollo, and they sing as foreknowing the good things their god hath in store for them'. The Greek philosopher Pythagoras said that the souls of all good poets passed into swans – but on the subject of bad poets, Coleridge wrote:

'Swans sing before they die; 'twere no bad thing
Should certain persons die before they sing.'

The fable is not true; only the so-called whistling swan of Iceland makes any vaguely musical sound. All the other varieties go through life – and death – with no more than a throaty croak.

Elephants never forget

There is apparently some truth in the belief that elephants never forget. In a recent experiment, Professor B. Rensch of Munster University in Germany showed that an elephant recalled a number of tests with a 73–100 per cent accuracy even after the lapse of a year. The experiment – in which the elephant was taught to associate certain symbols with

food – proved that although elephants are not very intelligent, and learn extremely slowly, once they have mastered something it will remain in their memories for a considerable length of time.

There is, however, no foundation in the belief that elephants are afraid of mice.

Earwigs enter human ears

Forficula auricularia, the most common species of earwig, is popularly supposed to have a peculiar liking for human ears, which it is said to enter at any opportunity and may damage with its pincers. In many other languages, the name for the earwig – *perce-oreille*, the French meaning 'ear piercer', and *ohrwurm*, the German meaning 'ear-worm' – seemingly reinforces the prevalence of the belief. In fact, earwigs are largely vegetarian, and unable to inflict much damage with their pincers. They have no special desire to enter human ears, though they may do so by accident, just as they may enter any other warm cavity. Once inside, they would probably be repelled by the bitter wax secreted there. The name may actually be derived from the ear-like shape of the hind wings of the insect.

Toads can be preserved alive in rocks

There are stories that toads have been discovered apparently imprisoned in rock cells for centuries. When released, they have hopped out none the worse for their ordeal. But it is not true. Like all living creatures, the toad needs air and food to survive. If one should be unlucky enough to become enclosed in rock it could feasibly live for a while *if* the rock were sufficiently porous to admit air and water, and perhaps tiny creatures; otherwise it would certainly die.

A bizarre 19th-century experiment proves this point. Dr William Buckland (1784–1856), a British geologist, built an

apparatus consisting of 24 stone cells covered on one side with glass panels. Twelve of the cells measured 12 × 5 in. and were composed of coarse oolitic limestone; 12 were 6 × 5 in. and made of compact siliceous sandstone. In these chambers Buckland placed 12 large and 12 small toads, evenly distributed between limestone and sandstone, and on November 26, 1825, he covered the apparatus with 3 ft of earth. Within 13 months, all the toads in the sandstone and the small toads in the limestone were dead. All the large toads in the limestone died within the next year. Apparently, the toads in limestone had access to air and water, and possibly food which had permeated through the rock; the large ones were also able to consume their own body bulk and thus live longer.

Cats suck the breath from sleeping babies

Many superstitions have surrounded the cat since ancient times. One which persists is the belief that they wilfully suck the breath from the mouths of sleeping babies, and thus suffocate them. Certainly, cats may like to settle in a warm cot, and a large cat may be heavier than a small baby, and so there have been cases where cats have smothered children by sleeping on their faces. But there is no evidence that they would or could draw the breath from the lungs of infants (the mouth of a cat could not cover a baby's mouth and nose simultaneously). A very simple precaution – placing a net across a child's cot or pram – will avoid the remote risk of suffocation.

Scorpions sting themselves to death

There is a legend that scorpions will sting themselves to death if they are surrounded by flames. It is certainly true that the poison of scorpions is extremely powerful, but in

common with other venomous animals they are completely immune to their own poison.

Camels carry water in their humps

The camel's capacity to survive without water for long periods in hot, dry deserts is well known, but probably greatly exaggerated. Under working conditions, camels can live for perhaps a week or ten days without drinking – possibly a little longer under exceptional circumstances. This ability has been explained as being due to the supply of water which the camel carries in its hump – but no such reservoir exists. The hump contains fat which the camel can draw on when no other food is available. In digesting it, water is produced which, together with water stored in small amounts in special stomach pouches, keeps the camel going in emergencies. Of course, other adaptations make the camel well suited to desert conditions, but there are many other animals which have a greater ability to survive without drinking water – the giraffe, and various species of antelope can go for months without drinking, because they can obtain sufficient water from the foliage they eat.

Rats desert a sinking ship

There is a widespread and ancient belief that rats have some sort of prophetic powers which will cause them to leave a sinking ship before it sets sail. Thus the sight of rats scurrying away from a vessel would make any sailor wary of its sea-worthiness. Clearly, there is some truth in the legend: if a ship is leaking badly before it sails, the rats which customarily live in the holds will seek refuge elsewhere – possibly leaving the ship altogether. But no rat can predict a disaster such as a collision, or striking an iceberg, before it happens. There is no evidence that rats ever left a doomed ship so long as the ship was seaworthy.

Snakes are charmed by music

Snakes have no ears and are unable to hear airborne sounds, including speech and music. Snakes are thus not 'charmed' by music, but may be influenced by the vibrations of the charmer's foot tapping on the ground, and once out of the basket will respond to the rhythmic swaying of his body and the pipe.

Ostriches can digest iron, and hide their heads in the sand

'I'll make thee eat iron like an ostrich'

(Shakespeare *Henry VI Part Two* IV.x.28)

As early as Shakespeare's time, the ostrich was depicted in prints with a horseshoe in its mouth, and it was popularly believed that it could eat anything. The ostrich is certainly powerful and voracious, and is stupid enough to swallow anything that looks like food. They also swallow small stones to help digestion. But numerous valuable ostriches in captivity have been killed by thoughtless people feeding them all sorts of curious objects. One at London Zoo which died after a busy holiday weekend was found to have eaten handkerchiefs, gloves, string, a pencil, a key and various coins.

Another myth concerning ostriches is that they hide their heads in the sand. Ostriches observed in the wild and in captivity have never been seen to do such a thing. When they hear the approach of an animal, they may bend their necks parallel with the ground and listen intently, but when in danger, like most other creatures, they run away.

Bulls are maddened by red rags

Scientific research has shown that bulls – like most mammals apart from monkeys and men – are colourblind. Matadors usually use red cloaks (perhaps because they do not show bloodstains), but they have also used other colours which have enraged the bulls to the same extent. It is the movement of the cloak, rather than its colour, which makes bulls angry.

Crocodiles shed tears

The phrase 'crocodile tears', meaning hypocritical grief, has been used in literature and everyday speech for hundreds of years. It stems from an early belief that the crocodile wept while devouring its victims. In his *De Proprietatibus Rerum*, the 13th-century English friar Bartholomaeus Anglicus wrote of the belief:

'If the crocodile findeth a man by the brim of the water,

or by the cliff, he slayeth him if he may, and then weepeth upon him and swalloweth him at last.'

The belief that the crocodile is unhappy at killing its prey is quite erroneous, of course, but crocodiles do shed 'tears' as a simple reflex action when their jaws are opened wide – as we might when we yawn. And so there is some basis to the old myth after all.

Flies walk on ceilings with foot-suckers

The foot of a housefly, like the feet of other insects when viewed under a microscope, does not resemble a rubber sucker in any way. The principle by which a fly can walk upside-down is simply one of adhesion by means of sticky pads. Each foot has a pair of these pads, or *pulvilli*, and a pair of hooks. The pads are covered with tiny hairs which are coated with a tacky substance with sufficient adhesive properties to enable the fly to walk at any angle on any surface. On rough surfaces, the hooks are used to provide a good grip.

SCIENCE

If it rains on St Swithin's Day, it will rain for 40 days

St Swithin, or Swithun, was Bishop of Winchester, and died in 862. His body was buried at his request outside his church where the 'rain of heaven' might fall on his grave. On July 15, 971, the legend goes, the monks attempted to move his remains inside their rebuilt cathedral, but the protesting saint started a 40 day storm. Since then, it has been a popular belief in England (although there are similar tales in other countries) that if it rains on St Swithin's day, it will rain for the next 40 days. But in the case of London, records do not support the belief; on average, if it is *dry* on St Swithin's Day, it rains on the next 17 days and produces a total of 3¼ in. whereas if it is *wet*, it rains on only the next 16 days, producing 2½ in. Since records started in 1860, no 40 day period has been wet throughout, but the following observations have been made. In 1924, despite bright sunshine on St Swithin's Day, 30 of the next 40 days were wet, while a torrential storm on the saint's day in 1913 was followed by only nine wet days in the next 40. (An observation which has not apparently been made is that the calendar has been altered since St Swithin's time, and so we may be taking the wrong anniversary as the base point for testing the accuracy of the legend.)

Quicksand sucks people down

Quicksand is a loose mixture of sand and water. As its density is greater than that of water, it will support a floating body at least as adequately as water alone. If a person steps into quicksand, the pressure of his feet is greater than the quicksand can support, and he will sink into it. In trying to lift one leg, a partial vacuum is formed around it by the resistance to flow of the sand particles; the leg is held and the downward pressure transferred to the other leg, so that it is gradually forced downwards. It is the frantic effort to escape which results in the tendency to sink, since the quicksand itself has no power to suck. Any suction noises would be made by the attempt to withdraw the trapped limbs, not by the sand pulling downwards. If a person does not panic, the quicksand will probably support a body at approximately armpit level.

Catgut is made from cats

A 19th-century description of the manufacture of catgut begins, 'Take the entrails of a sheep . . .' No mention is made of cats, and it is highly unlikely that the catgut used for tennis rackets and violin strings has ever been made from

the gut of cats. Today it is made from the intestines of sheep, horses and some other animals – but not cats.

The origin of the word is obscure. It could have come from 'cattlegut', or may have resulted from a confusion between 'kit' and kitten, a kit being a small violin, which would no doubt have had catgut strings. The *Oxford English Dictionary* includes, without suggesting it to be true, the joking story that the origin may derive from the caterwauling sound a violin may produce. Even by Shakespeare's time people were aware that cats played no part in the manufacture of catgut:

'Is it not strange that sheeps' guts should hale souls out of men's bodies?' wrote Shakespeare (*Much Ado About Nothing* II.iii) of the emotional effect a stringed instrument can produce.

Bullets get red-hot in flight

'Hot lead' is a vivid description of the gunfights of the Wild West, but 'hot guns' might be more accurate. Although a gun barrel gets hot in action, a bullet is cooled considerably as it passes through the air. A bullet retrieved immediately after being fired is not hot, though the force of impact may distort the lead and give it the appearance of having melted.

The Arctic is an icy waste

It is generally assumed that the further north a person travels, the colder it becomes. The Arctic is thus generally thought to be immensely cold, permanently dark, totally devoid of all forms of life and often snowing.

The truth is that the North Pole is never as cold as some parts of the USA. In 1954 the temperature at Roger's Pass, Montana, dropped to −57°C (−70°F), but temperatures below −46°C (−50°F) are rare at the North Pole. Virginia has more snow than the Arctic lowlands, and the world record for snowfall is held by Mt Rainier in Washington State, with 1000 in. in one year. It is never totally dark in the extreme north, due to the refraction of light on the snow – according to one authority 'the number of hours yearly during which print can be read out of doors is as great in the Arctic as in the Tropics'. Above the Arctic Circle in the summer, temperatures of 32°C (90°F) and above are recorded, and hundreds of species of flowering plants and grasses flourish, providing food for large numbers of animals. All sorts of domestic vegetables and flowers will thrive, including the potato and roses; and the Arctic seas teem with life.

Drowning people go down three times

The idea that a drowning man rises to the surface twice before sinking for the third and last time is a long-established myth. If the water and the swimmer remain calm, a man can float fairly comfortably, because the specific gravity of a body is lower than that of water – especially of sea-water. But if the water is rough or the man is a non-swimmer, or a swimmer who panics, water may be washed into the lungs, and repeated movements may eventually result in submergence. As the man struggles to the surface for breath, more water is drawn into the lungs, and the process of submergence may be repeated several times before death from drowning occurs – but there is certainly no set number.

Red sky at night, shepherds' delight

Research has shown that as many as half the common weather proverbs may be at least partly correct. For instance, 'Red sky at night, shepherds' delight. Red sky in the morning, shepherds' warning', is usually true. A pale red sky in the evening, caused by sunlight refracted through haze, is generally a sign of good weather the following day. A heavier red sky seen beneath a cloud layer, whether early or late in the day, is often a portent of stormy weather. The belief is ancient, and equally applicable to most countries – it is actually mentioned in the Bible (Matthew 16.ii) *And the Pharisees and Sadducees came, and to test him they asked him to show them a sign from heaven. He answered them, 'When it is evening, you say, "It will be fair weather; for the sky is red." And in the morning, "It will be stormy today, for the sky is red and threatening". . .'*

Watches are damaged by turning the hands backwards

The hands and winder of a watch are not connected to the rest of the mechanism in such a way that the action of winding the hands forwards or backwards operates the entire train of cogs. If they were, the winding of the hands through, say, one hour in a simple twist of the winder lasting one second, would force the escapement to work at 3600 times its usual speed. It does not matter which way the hands of a watch are turned. But care should be taken with some striking clocks which may be constructed on a different principle and may be damaged by backward winding.

Lightning zigzags, and 'never strikes twice'

Although widely published photographs of lightning clearly show it to follow a pattern resembling a river with tributaries, artists persist in representing it in the form of zigzags which, however graphic, are quite inaccurate.

Ignorance of the nature of lightning has led to a wealth of superstition, the chief of which in Western culture is that lightning never strikes twice in the same place. In fact, lightning generally strikes prominent buildings, and as long as they remain prominent, lightning will tend to strike them. The Empire State building was struck 68 times during its first ten years, and numerous English churches have been struck on more than one occasion; St Botolph's, Boston, Lincolnshire, was hit four times between 1865 and 1908.

For this reason, high buildings have a lightning conductor, a copper rod, protruding above the highest point. As copper is a good conductor of electricity it is more likely to be hit by lightning, and it then carries the electrical charge down into the earth where it is dissipated.

A secondhand car with 'one lady owner' is a good buy

A car owned by a 'little old lady', and used only for shopping trips and visiting nearby friends, may be far from a prudent buy. The most serious wear to a car's engine occurs when it is cold and driven 'on choke'. Unburnt petrol in the cylinder washes away the protective film of oil on the cylinder walls causing increased wear, and condensation causes corrosion.

If the car is used only for brief journeys, there is every chance that the engine is *never* functioning at its optimum temperature, and it may be more badly worn than one which has covered three times the mileage.

THE LAW

Shopkeepers must sell goods at the price marked in the window

In law, the display of goods is merely an 'invitation to treat', or an invitation to the customer to offer to buy. Buying something in a shop involves making a contract, and for a contract to exist the customer must make his offer (by saying what he wants, for instance), the shopkeeper must accept, and the two parties must confer a benefit on each other (by exchanging the goods for money). Until all three actions have taken place the shopkeeper need not sell at all. If he demands a higher price than the one advertised however, he may be liable under the Trade Descriptions Act.

If a condemned man survived three attempts to hang him, or was afterwards revived, he would be freed

It was once held by common consent, though never by law, that it was permissible to remove men from the gallows at public hangings and attempt to revive them. If they survived they were entitled to go free. Such attempts were sometimes successful, but there are also records of executions, such as that of the housebreaker and escaper Jack Sheppard, when the crowds were so dense that all attempts at rescue failed.

A notable case which has furthered the idea of hanging as a game of chance was the attempted execution of John Lee in 1885. He had been found guilty of murdering his employer Emma Keyse by cutting her throat and then setting fire to her house. On February 23 at Exeter Jail, three attempts were made to hang him, each of which failed because the boards of the trapdoor had been warped by rain the previous night.

His sentence was commuted to life imprisonment, and Lee was released 23 years later. He emigrated to the USA where he died in 1933. The commuting of his sentence was a humane gesture by Sir William Harcourt, the Home Secretary, and not an established law of the land. The sentence, in the days of hanging, was that the prisoner should be 'hanged by the neck until dead' – with no provisos for a sporting chance if the equipment failed, or if he could afterwards be revived.

The death penalty has been abolished in Britain

Capital punishment for murder no longer exists in Britain. However, there are two crimes for which hanging is still technically the penalty. They are:

Treason Under the Treason Acts 1790 and 1814 a person may be executed for such offences as conspiring to kill the

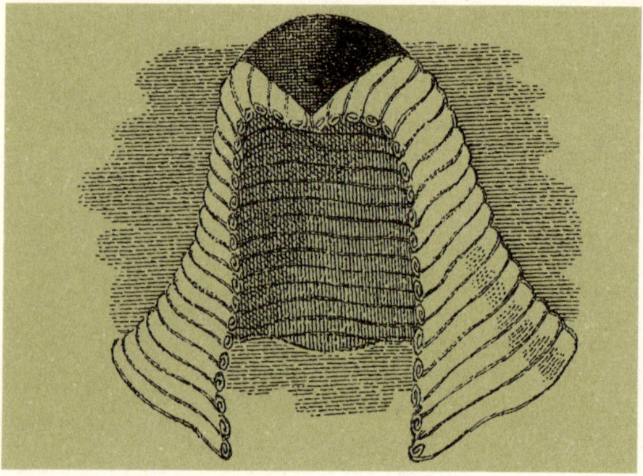

king or queen or their eldest son and heir; violating the king's wife, the eldest unmarried daughter or the wife of the heir; warring against the king in his kingdom or adhering to his enemies abroad; killing the chancellor, treasurer or king's justices; and attempting by force or in writing to hinder succession to the Crown.

Piracy with violence This section of the Piracy Act 1837 has not been repealed.

Arson in a naval dockyard Until 1971, when the law was changed by the Criminal Damage Act, setting fire to ships in H.M. Dockyards was also punishable by death.

Madame Tussaud's offers £100 to anyone who will spend the night in the Chamber of Horrors

This popular belief was promoted by Charles Dickens in his magazine *Household Words* over a hundred years ago, when

he invited young men to seek permission to spend the night at the Chamber of Horrors and to write down their impressions of the experience. To advertise the play *The Whip* in 1909, the Drury Lane Theatre produced handbills offering £100 reward to anyone who would stay the night in the Chamber of Horrors, on the condition that they 'shall not smoke or drink or read during the 12 hours'. No one apparently came forward, or if they did Madame Tussaud's turned them away. Madame Tussaud's have never made the offer themselves or encouraged anyone who has tried to take it up. But the belief has become so widely established that the company still receives an average of two letters a week from people offering to accept the 'challenge'.

Some versions of the old story tell of men who have actually spent the night in the Chamber and been reduced to gibbering idiots. The Chamber originally contained death masks of victims of the French Revolution, including Louis XVI and Marie Antoinette, together with a guillotine.

Modern 'horrors' that have been added include models of the mass murderer John Christie in his kitchen at 10 Rillington Place, and John George Haig, the acid-bath murderer who sent his clothes to Madame Tussaud's on the eve of his execution.

A woman may re-marry after the disappearance of her husband for seven years

Until 1938, a spouse (either man or woman) could, after seven years' absence and presuming the other to be dead, quite legally marry again. But the custom involved a major risk. The second marriage was, in legal terms, regarded as 'presumptively valid'. If the missing spouse reappeared, the second marriage was held to be 'conclusively void', which might involve considerable hardships.

Under the Matrimonial Causes Acts 1937 and 1965, the High Court may now issue a decree of presumption of death if there are no reasonable grounds for supposing the spouse to be alive after seven years. The petitioner may then enter into a second marriage in the certainty that the first marriage is no longer valid.

INDEX

Part of the material in this booklet
is drawn from *The Natural History of Nonsense*,
by Bergen Evans, published in the USA
by Alfred A. Knopf Inc., and in
England by Michael Joseph Ltd

Printing and binding by
W. S. Cowell Limited,
Ipswich, Suffolk